How to Invest in the Stock Market Maximize Your Profits in The Millionaire Market

Smit Chacha

Copyright © 2021 Smit Chacha

All rights reserved.

ISBN: 9798542883779

DEDICATION

I want to dedicate this book to every single stock market newcomer and experienced investor. This book contains all the essential tips and guides in how to invest in the stock market and maximize your profits.

CONTENTS

How to Invest in the Stock Market – Maximize Your Profits in The Millionaire Market 3

How Stock Market Works 5

Is it Safe to Invest in the Stock Market? 7

What is Market Volatility? 8

Stock Market Future Trends (Goldmines) 10

Studying the Market 11

Media Platforms 13

Technical Analyses 14

Spread betting Vs Stock Market Plus Online Brokers 14

Your Budget and Portfolio 16

Historical Data Matters 17

Quick Profit Vs Big Long-Term Profit 18

Trading Robots and Human Trading 18

The Pros and Cons of Stock Market 19

How to be a Successful Investor in the Stock Market 20

Pitfalls to Avoid in the Stock Market 21

Bullish and Bearish Market Trends 22

Seasonal Trends 23

The Graphs 24

Example of Income Statement and Balanced Sheet 25

Degiro and Other Brokers Fees Comparison 29

ACKNOWLEDGMENTS

I have been investing in the stock market for over 10 years and I have been successful in doing my online trades and investments. I believe now it is time to give something back. I want to share my personal experience as a stock market investor.

How to Invest in the Stock Market – Maximize Your Profits in The Millionaire Market

Hi,

My name is Smit Chacha and I am a stock market investor with over 10 years' experience in trading in the stock market. I have seen the ups and downs of the market trend and was able to maximize my profits during the pandemics and during the booming years. Trading in stocks is very different than trading on currencies or commodities. I have been a daily trader in forex and made huge profits in the stocks trading shares.

The aim of this book is to teach you how to trade on the stock market and find the goldmine and avoid the most common pitfalls. Trading is easy and fun when you are making huge profits and this is the main focus of this master class. Finding the right moment to trade in the key for any investor.

There are my companies to trade within the stock market, some will succeed in huge gains while others will not last long and this is what as a trader you should be aware of. Making the right choice to trade in the proper timeframe will define how successful you will be. Timing is the key.

I have seen many huge companies fall of the stock market during the pandemics and many have even got bankrupt. Avoid these common pitfalls and save your money. Invest in a company that has a strong portfolio data. For instance, During the 2020/2021 corona or covid-19 pandemic many rich companies fall, including Rolls Royce, EasyJet, Lloyds and many others. EasyJet had a pandemic plan and they set over 2 billion a side for the pandemic. This made the company very much reliable to trade and make profit. Cineworld for instance went from making profit into to a long tail of losses and their share price fall dramatically. EasyJet share prices also fall during the pandemic however because EasyJet had a pre plan they are likely to recover and make profit.

The FTSE100 during the covid 19 pandemic alongside other European, American and Asian Indices fall dramatically and many huge companies went near bankrupt.

No one was prepared for this downturn many investors lost huge amounts, specially those who were trading before the pandemic. Those lucky ones (included me) made decent profits in this downtrend. I was able to maximize my profits during the pandemic.

How Stock Market Works

The stock market works in the clockwise condition. There are many markets to trade on. Asian, European and American. They are timely defined and the trading last during the trading hours. I have focused this book on the European Market, especially the UK market. The trading hours of this market starts from 8am and last till 4:30pm. During this trading session you can buy and sell stocks or shares and invest in the market.

The London Stock Exchange in composed with many Indices such as FTSE100, FTSE250 FTSE350 and many others.

Generally speaking, the stock market Indices work sector wise and each sector is composed with many share companies. When the overall data is bullish the Indices is high and when the data is bearish the Indices is low.

As I said earlier, we are only focusing on UK market in this book but the techniques and analyses applies to all markets around the world.

Each company has a market cap of stocks and they are traded on daily bases. When people buy a stock in large quantities the price goes up and when people start to sell the stock the price falls. This is the bases of stock market.

Now companies that are in the stock market are bound to publish their revenue data and you can check on the londonstockexchange.com website. Just type the name of the company or their company code and you can check their last 5 years transaction data under fundamentals. This applies to all the stock market in the world. For UK is the londonstockexchange.com for other countries is their own stock market website.

USA has Dow Jones, Nasdaq, etc. The German has their Dax, the French with their Cac, and there are many more around the world. Just go to their stock exchange website and get all the details of the company and figure it out for yourself if this is the company you want to trade with.

There is also a company house in each country where you can check the latest tax recorded data. Plus, there are many channels including social media where these companies share their common interest with the investor. This news sharing makes the market very much dynamic and tradable.

For instance, when an airline company such as EasyJet share a travel news data their share prices get very volatile and this applies to all tourism and travel industry and their trading partners. Sudden events such as changing their chairman or CEO for better or for worse matters a lot in the stock market.

The stock market can be a gold mine if you know when and a where to trade. For example, the Tesla car company that produces electric cars when they first started on the stock market their shares where under $30 each and in their pick period roughly after 4 years the company shares were trading at $850 each! Which means if you invested on Tesla early on with only $5000 you would get roughly 166 shares and sell it on the pick period you would made at least $141000 minus stamp duty and your brokers fees.

Is it Safe to Invest in the Stock Market?

This is the most common question people ask me. Is it safe to invest in the stock market? Let me explain why you should invest on the stock market. First the companies that you will invest are public limited and they will share their revenue date with you. So, it is up to your which company you want to invest. A well-established company with lots of profit in the last 5 or 10 plus years have a better valued price and a good choice to invest. A company with many losses and debts are very volatile and they have the risk to the de-indexed from the stock market. As the company went to administrate or in other words bankrupt.

A solid company will also give dividends to their share holder. This can be in a form of cash of bonus shares. The company will publish a data when and how many dividends they will give to their investors. Some companies give once a year while others up to 4 times a year. A dividend will only be cashed on if you hold the company share for longer. Generally speaking, when dividends are published the share value of the company will rise and it is up to you to cash out on the dividend date of keep the shares and cash out the dividend amount.

For example, a company with lots of profits in the last 5 years published a dividend date of £1.5 per share and the market price of the company is £500, this is just an example, the due date of the dividend the company share price jumps 10% and you have 10 shares with this company it is up to you to cash out £550 or keep the shares for more time and risk the market volatility and cash out the dividend amount of £15.

This process happens automatically if you do not cash out you will receive the dividend amount the very next day in your account. Some companies offer bonus shares for example you have 1000 shares and you do not cash out your shares on the dividend date the next day you will receive bonus shares. It could be 2000 in total or just 50%.

What is Market Volatility?

Market volatility simply means the ups and down of the market movement. All the highs and lows that happen in the market is called market volatility. And this happens whenever there is a news about the industry or about the particular company.

There are many channels where you can find this news data. From their company website, social media and television. Any news that affects the industry makes the market very volatile. A sudden spark in the market can make you a fortune or lose money and this applies to all the markets and Indices around the world.

As the news data arrives the market starts to get fluctuated and thus volatility starts. In a breaking news the market can be very volatile and can jump over 10% up or down even in the FTSE100.

EasyJet shares for example on the breaking news of corona virus and quarantine requirements set by each country governments their shares went from trading £9.60 to £7.21 in just 3 days! Rolls Royce shares also plunged over 10% and where drop from £1.10 to £0.89 in just 2 days and many other huge companies drops their share value in the covid 19 pandemic.

For me was an opportunity to make huge amount during this pandemic crisis I made lots of profit in this timeframe. Many lost huge amounts as they were unaware of the pandemic that was ahead and they did not sell their shares early. I on the other hand had my portfolio neat and clean and started investing straight after the pandemic hit.

For any investor timing is the key investing in the right time makes a huge difference and this is what I want to teach you. Invest in the stock market in correct time. Do not invest when the trend is already too high. Invest when the trend is low and has a potential to do higher.

Stock Market Future Trends (Goldmines)

Stock market is a gold mine as I said earlier, I missed the Tesla running price when it was trading at only $30 per share and within a few years it jumps to $850 per share. This was a great investment at the time. I missed but many turn multimillionaires with just these shares.

Petrol and diesel cars a thing of the past the future is electric cars and this made Tesla very rich and competitive. In just 3 to 4 years, they become a market leader and their shares were trading above $500 consistently in 2021.

Samsung and Apple are another future trend that got very huge success, despite Nokia being the market leader of the past mobile phone era, they did not predict the future. The future was smart phones and therefore Nokia become a thing of the past.

Cryptocurrency such as Bitcoin is also a thing of the future and made huge success in the 21st century. Who would thought that in future we will see a new currency in the market and Bitcoin once trading at $250 jumped to trade over $30000 in 2021, a huge success and a thing of the future.

Sci-fi movies are also where many see where the future is heading, watch these movies and if you thing it is durable and there is a market value for this earlier and they do not invest just a little bit and who knows in just a few years you might see the fruits of your investment turning into gold.

A good trend that looks like it gone get success in future is VR, although not a huge success now in 2021 but who knows what the future is for this type of technology. The drawback of this kind of investment in 2021 is that they are at least 14 companies registered in the stock market producing VR technology. Now which one will turn into gold? We do not know that yet. But keeping an eye on this trend can make you very rich in the future.

Studying the Market

A good way to study the market or should I say the companies that are registered in the stock market is by checking their dividend data. We have touched a little bit about this earlier, here we go into detail.

If the company is making profit, then the company will issue dividends to their investors. And this is where you know if you should invest in this company or not. A company with losses of debts are not able to provide dividends to their investors. And these are the companies to be aware of.

Cineworld a FTSE250 company there are many Cineworld cinemas around the globe. You might think it is a profitable company to be invested on. Look again Cineworld has lots of debts and are unable to provide dividends to their investors in 2021. Therefore, this is a company to be aware of.

EasyJet probably will not provide a dividend data on year 2021, however this company has a history to give lots of dividends in the last 10 plus years. They also have budgeted 2 billion pounds a side for the pandemic. A profitable company and this is where you should consider investing compared to Cineworld.

Dividends giving companies are generally safer to invest as they are making profits on yearly bases. Another way to study the market is to find the fundamentals or the income balance sheet. Study the balance sheet check if the company made any loss in the last 5 to 10 years and if the company has any debts or not.

Generally speaking, a company that are giving dividends are debt free and making profit on consistent bases. And this is why many investors want to invest. The drawback of these companies is that their market value will not be very volatile and the investment you made will be profitable but not has volatile than those companies that are running under debt management.

Cineworld for example a company with many debts and still people find it very much tradable because it is very volatile the shares of this company can be up to 35% volatile in just 5 days of trading. You might buy a share trading at £0.65 today and tomorrow it is trading at £0.77

or vice versa. The volatility of this company makes it very much tradable, however it is also very much riskier as this company as a potential to collapse because of their huge debts.

Media Platforms

A good way to be a stock market investor is to follow the companies you trade with in Twitter and other social media platforms. These companies many times will give you a hint or a tip of when and where to invest in this share stock market. Newsbreaks are generally followed in this online media platform alongside television.

Many times, you will notice a newsbreak in Twitter and not followed in the TV, this is why you should always follow companies in their social media platform to become an intelligent investor.

I follow every single company that I invest in the social media and I noticed many times general tips that they share on their time and makes my investment a lot smarter and a lot more profitable and this is a tip I want to stress out in this book. Follow your investment in every single department. Online and offline and become a smarter and intelligent investor.

Bloomberg, CNBC, BBC, etc. these are the news channels that you should watch for any breaking news of your investment. As I said many times that news plays a critical role in the stock market. It makes that market volatile and dynamic to trade. And trading at the right time makes that big difference in earning a few pounds to few thousand pounds more!

Technical Analyses

If you are a forex or commodity trader you will be familiar with this term. However, in the stock market technical analyses do not work in the daily trading days. Newsbreaks and the volume of trades are what determents the market ups and downs. If there is a huge volume of trade the market will go slightly high and if there is a huge volume of sales the market will drop. The newsbreaks will determine how high the market volatile will be.

What I mean to say is that doing a Fibonacci on the stock market will not work. It only works on commodities and currencies not on shares and stocks.

Spread betting Vs Stock Market Plus Online Brokers

There is a huge difference in trading shares then doing spread betting. If you spread bet you are trading on the actual spread and your profits or losses comes from the difference of the spread. The stock market or trading shares is difference, here you are actually buying the share not the spread. And the profit or losses comes from the value of the share times quantity you have bought.

There is no timeframe to buy of sell shares as long as the share company is registered to the stock market. The expenses are based on your broker plus stamp duty that everyone has to pay. The actual brokerage fees may vary, the stamp duty fees are standard to any broker.

I trade with Degiro.co.uk they are an online broker with an online platform and with a mobile app where you can trade on the run. The fees are very reasonable only £1.75 per trade plus stamp duty on UK shares and £0.50 per trade plus stamp duty on USA shares and they trade on the global market. Just go to their website for more details.

I have been trading with Degiro.co.uk for a number of years and never had any problem. They also have a phone number and a great customer service team to help you in your investments. There are loads of brokers out there, Degiro.co.uk is the broker I trade with. Just check their website and if you think this is the broker for you then go ahead.

Do a Google search for stock market share brokers and you will find a ton of them. Do your own research on the brokerage and start trading on the stock market.

Your Budget and Portfolio

If you are thinking in investing in the stock market, make a self-budget in how much you can afford to lose. Ideally your investment should come from your savings. And you should diversify your portfolio. A portfolio means the number of stocks your have from a number of companies. Do not invest everything in just one company, diversify it and spread it for as many stocks you can. To avoid disappointment.

Diversifying your portfolio will minimize your losses in the long run. Simply because you are diversifying your portfolio you can manage your investments. What it means that when a stock is high and others are low you can sell the highs and keep the lows for future. If you invest everything in just one stock you will have to wait for longer and the risk is too high.

Have a budget in how much you can afford to lose. Stock market is relatively safe if you know when and where you are investing. The stocks with profitable dividends are likely to be the best choice to invest in the stock market.

Historical Data Matters

Remembering the history always is a good idea and gives you experience as an investor. History can repeat and in stocks are likely to happen. An experienced investor will always remember history. If something happens in the stock market in the past where the trend of the news where similar the chances are the numbers will also be similar. Remembering the past will make you an experienced investor in the stock market.

An experienced investor is likely to profit more in the stock market than a newcomer. Over time you will notice certain happenings in the market and you will become an experienced invertor. This happens after starting investing for a certain period. You will automatically notice the ups and downs of the market. And your experience will determine how successful investor you will be.

Keeping an eye on the news channels and on the stocks, you invest you will automatically self-educate in when and where to invest in the stock market. Just give it some time and all of these will be automatic for you.

Quick Profit Vs Big Long-Term Profit

In the stock market you will also notice that sometimes it is better to be a short time daily investor and make quick profit rather than wait for longer and make huge profit. If you notice that a trend is happening, a certain newsbreak and the stocks gain over 10% in just one day, my advice is to make a quick profit and reinvest when the market is low.

A quick profit example, EasyJet was trading at £9.60 and with a news break the stocks jumped to £10.12 this is around 10% gains and a quick way to exit the market. I have invested over £25000 worth of shares (2604 shares to be precise) and in just one day I profited over £1350 minus brokerage fees and stamp duty.

Now I could wait for longer as the covid pandemic neutralizes and the shares are up and running their previous regular price of over £18 per share. However, I choose to take a quick profit and exit the market quickly. And I will reinvest on this stock when the price is under £9.60. And so, it was just 2 weeks later.

Trading Robots and Human Trading

If you do a little search online on trading robots you will notice that the market is filled with these. My advice is do not waste your time on these robotic software as they do not work. There is nothing like a human investor and human touch. Do not be a lazy investor and risk your assets on a software that do not work.

This software is built with a historical graph and see patterns when and where the market was at the similar price range and auto invest your assets on these historical graphs. And they not always time work. Do not be a lazy investor. It is your money do not let a software ruin it. Use your human brain to invest in the stock market.

The software gives you signals to invest use it as a tool to keep an eye on, do not use it to totally invest your assets. Your money is better invested when you know what you are doing. Do not let a software make decisions, use your human brain to make decisions on stock market investments.

The Pros and Cons of Stock Market

Here are some pros and cons in investing in the stock market:

Pros:

- It is a real investment and a business model
- It is your own investment portfolio
- You do not need a bank or a place to invest your money
- You can do it online or on a mobile app
- You get dividends on quality stocks
- You are free to invest in any market or stock you want and there is no limit in how much you want to invest

Cons:

- It is an investment and there are risks as companies may get de-listed from the market due to long term losses or debts
- There are brokerage fees and stamp duties to consider

There you have it my quick overview of pros and cons of investing in the stock market. It is all up to you if you want to start this investment model as a business. All you need is a laptop, internet and smart phone. You can invest in any market or stock at any trading time. There is no limit in how much you want to invest. It is up to you. The market is risky and it could be a goldmine if you know when and where to invest in the proper timely manner.

How to be a Successful Investor in the Stock Market

It takes time to be successful in any field, the money experience you have the more successful you will be in any field, including stock market. Keeping an eye on the daily news trends will determine how successful you will be. And this will happen only when you start investing in the market.

My advice is to start with a low amount something like £5000 and see your investment grow. With this amount you many find it like a part-time income or full time depending on your investment. My portfolio of stocks is well over £50000 and my diversity of shares made me very profitable and successful in the stock market. I remember when I first started investing and my first investment or should I say my first portfolio of shares where under £5000 and I made around £400 by the end of the month (after all the brokerage fees and stamp duties).

Anyone can invest in the stock market all you need is some savings a laptop, internet and a smart phone. If you have that why not start investing in the stock market! Stock market can be a goldmine as many with limited capital become multimillionaires in a short time and so can you!

Pitfalls to Avoid in the Stock Market

As an experienced investor here are my tips to avoid the most common pitfalls for a newcomer:

Do not start investing without a proper research on the market, check the fundamentals of the company. Check their revenue, their income statement and see if they are in debt or did, they made any losses in the last 5 to 10 years. If they are in debt and made some losses avoid them as a newcomer. As a newcomer invest on stocks that are giving you dividends and these companies are making profit and they are ideal candidates for a newcomer to invest.

Cineworld for example it is a very well-known cinema company with hundreds of cinemas around the world. As a newcomer you might fancy this stock to be invested. Now if you check their income and balance sheet you will notice that Cineworld alongside Rolls Royce are in huge debts for now and they made huge losses in the last 5 years. Avoid this stock as a newcome and invest on stocks that are far safer. You will make profit in the stock market on dividend giving stocks. The highs will be limited; however, profit will be seen compared to other stocks.

Bullish and Bearish Market Trends

Generally speaking, a bullish market simply means that the market price is raising, while a bearish market means the price is falling. Ideally you should buy a stock on a bearish market and sell it on a bullish market, this is how the stock market works.

The market indices are an indicator of which sector of the market is bullish or bearish. This happens throughout the trading session of the market. In UK the market starts at 8 am and ends at 4:30 pm. And during this session the market could be bullish or bearish. The trend keeps changing and this makes the stock market very much tradable and dynamic.

As an investor you must see where the trend is heading, buy a stock at low price and sell it on a higher price and keep the profit with you. Also keep in mind that your expenses are covered including the brokerage fees and the stamp duty. If you are in profit why not sell the stock and keep the profits with you and reinvest when the market in bearish. This is how the stock market works.

Seasonal Trends

Each sector of the market with time you will find some seasonal trends. The ups and lows of the market trend matching the seasons of trading. For instance, in the summer the travel industry will have a higher price, this is seen as a seasonal trend. The automobile industry when it became an electric car invention this trend also impacted the market.

With experience you will notice these seasonal trends and you will become a much more successful investor of the stock market. A good example if when the pandemic started the medical sector also impacted the market trend. And this will always be the case. Keep an eye on the news and breaking news and this is how a successful investor invest in the stock market.

Become a smarter and intelligent investor by checking the seasons of trading and by keeping an eye on the news and breaking news. These trends are temporal and the best time to invest. As I said when and where to invest in the proper timely manner makes a successful stock market investor.

The Graphs

Check the stock graphs and make notes why the market has fallen and why the market has raised at that particular point. Check the news and events of that timeframe and predict when in future this temporal trend will happen. Everyday the news is different, however the trends remain the same. Either it is seasonal or a breaking news event. Or even a pandemic of 2020/2021.

History will always repeat itself in the stock market and as an experienced investor over time you will notice these ups and downs Coe siding with your past findings. An experienced investor will always make more profit than a newcome and experience takes time.

After some time, all of these will make sense to you and all of these will become automatic for you. You will start to invest the smart and intelligent ways with time.

Never forget the past as it is a tool to predict the future of the stock market. The more detailed you go in stocks the more time you give on your research you will be more successful in this stock market.

Example of Income Statement and Balanced Sheet

Here is an example of income statement and balance sheet (of Rolls Royce):

Income statement	31.12.15 (£m)	31.12.16 (£m)	31.12.17 (£m)	31.12.18 (£m)	31.12.19 (£m)
Total Revenue	13,725.00	14,955.00	16,307.00	15,729.00	16,587.00
Cost of Revenue					
Gross Profit					
Operating Expenses					
Depreciation & Amortisation					
Other Operating Expenses					
Operating profit	1,309.00	73.00	1,954.00	1,165.00	956.00
Net Interest		63.00	56.00		
Other non operating income/expense					
Pre tax profits (from continued & discontinued)	60.00	4,753.00	4,766.00	7,853.00	995.00
Taxes					
After tax profits (from continued & discontinued)	16.00	4,149.00	4,077.00	2,397.00	1,415.00
Below line adjustments					
Net profit (from continued & discontinued)	84.00	4,832.00	4,208.00	2,303.00	1,311.00
Non controlling interests					
Equity holders of parent company		4,017.00	4,207.00	2,461.00	1,315.00
Continued EPS - Basic					
Continued & Discontinued EPS - Basic					
Dividend per share					

Balance sheet	31.12.15 (£m)	31.12.16 (£m)	31.12.17 (£m)	31.12.18 (£m)	31.12.19 (£m)
Total Assets	22,324.00	25,538.00	30,002.00	31,857.00	32,266.00
Non current assets	10,209.00	12,680.00	15,467.00	15,707.00	15,212.00
Current assets	12,115.00	12,858.00	14,995.00	16,091.00	16,954.00
Total liabilities	17,310.00	23,676.00	23,835.00	32,931.00	35,642.00
Non-current liabilities	9,135.00	11,268.00	12,987.00	17,982.00	20,628.00
Current liabilities	8,175.00	9,316.00	10,925.00	14,951.00	14,979.00
Net assets	5,014.00	1,862.00	6,167.00	1,014.00	-3,376.00
Total Equity	5,016.00	1,864.00	6,170.00	1,052.00	-3,354.00
Shareholders Funds	5,014.00	1,862.00	6,167.00	1,074.00	3,376.00
Non controlling interests				22.00	22.00

Ratios - based on IFRS	31.12.15	31.12.16	31.12.17	31.12.18	31.12.19

As you can see Rolls Royce despite being a huge and well-know company it is running on losses. And there is not dividend data for the past 5 years. As a newcome this is a stock that you should avoid.

Now let's check EasyJet income statement and balance sheet:

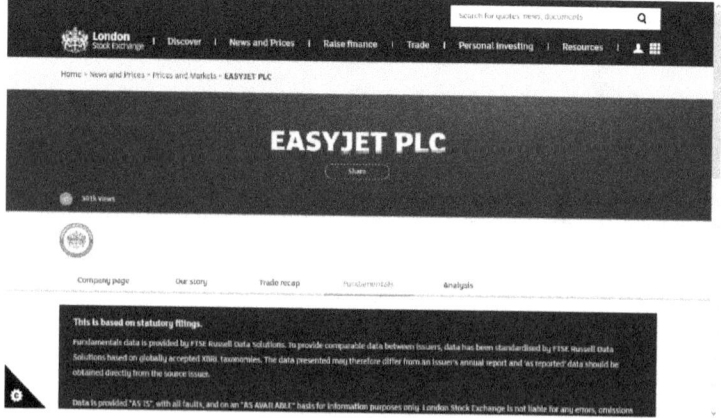

How to Invest in the Stock Market – Maximize Your Profits in The Millionaire Market

Income statement	30.09.16 (£m)	30.09.17 (£m)	30.09.18 (£m)	30.09.19 (£m)	30.09.20 (£m)
Total Revenue	4,669.00	5,047.00	5,898.00	6,385.00	3,009.00
Cost of Revenue	-	-	-	-	-
Gross Profit	-	-	-	-	-
Operating Expenses					
Depreciation & Amortisation					
Other Operating Expenses					
Operating profit	498.00	408.00	468.00	468.00	899.00
Net Interest	-3.00	-23.00	-24.00	-38.00	-44.00
Other non-operating income/expense	-	-	-	-	-
Pre tax profits (from continued & discontinued)	495.00	385.00	445.00	430.00	-1,273.00
Taxes					
After tax profits (from continued & discontinued)	427.00	305.00	358.00	349.00	-1,079.00
Below the adjustments					
Net profit (from continued & discontinued)	427.00	305.00	358.00	349.00	-1,079.00
Non-controlling Interests	-	-	-	-	-
Net profit (from continued & discontinued)	427.00	305.00	358.00	349.00	-1,079.00
Non-controlling Interests					
Equity holders of parent company	427.00	305.00	358.00	349.00	-1,079.00
Continued EPS - Basic	108.40p	77.40p	90.90p	86.80p	264.90p
Continued & Discontinued EPS - Basic	108.40p	77.40p	90.90p	86.80p	264.90p
Dividend per share	53.80p	40.90p	53.80p	43.90p	

Balance sheet	30.09.16 (£m)	30.09.17 (£m)	30.09.18 (£m)	30.09.19 (£m)	30.09.20 (£m)
Total Assets	5,505.00	5,971.00	6,985.00	8,163.00	8,473.00
Non current assets	4,051.00	4,237.00	5,304.00	5,644.00	5,418.00
Current assets	1,454.00	1,734.00	1,381.00	2,113.00	2,061.00
Total liabilities	2,792.00	3,169.00	3,736.00	5,178.00	6,574.00
Non current liabilities	1,520.00	1,499.00	1,420.00	2,349.00	3,248.00
Current liabilities	1,272.00	1,670.00	2,368.00	2,668.00	3,326.00
Net assets	2,712.00	2,802.00	3,250.00	2,985.00	1,899.00
Total Equity	2,712.00	2,802.00	3,250.00	2,985.00	1,899.00
Shareholders funds	2,712.00	2,802.00	3,250.00	2,985.00	1,899.00

Ratios - based on IFRS	30.09.16	30.09.17	30.09.18	30.09.19	30.09.20
PE ratio	9.29	15.72	14.46	12.90	
PEG	-0.43	-0.15	0.85	-5.13	
Earnings per Share Growth	-22.3%	-28.62%	17.44%	-7.15%	
Dividend Cover	2.01	1.92	1.55	2.07	
Revenue Per Share	1,181.79p	1,270.80p	1,490.95p	1,626.60p	737.29p
Pre tax Profit per share	125.49p	97.49p	112.99p	109.41p	-311.87p
Operating Margin	12.67%	8.00%	7.88%	7.33%	29.89%
Return on Capital Employed	15.07%	11.16%	11.13%	15.47%	18.33%
Dividend yield	4.64%	4.15%	4.46%	3.47%	
Dividend per Share Growth	36.62%	7.14%	23.52%	29.39%	-128.9%
Net Asset Value per share incl intangibles	552.02p	565.17p	682.02p	618.53p	287.97p

As you can see EasyJet only made a loss last year due to

pandemic and they are still giving you a dividend. As a newcomer this is the stock you should consider investing in. This is just an example and the trend may change in the future. By the time you read this book the income statement and balance sheet can be different. This example is made from 23/07/2021.

I am not encouraging you to invest on any of the above stocks, I am simply comparing the both companies balance sheet and income sheet and giving you, my findings. As an experienced investor I would stay away from Rolls Royce and keep an eye on EasyJet shares and stocks to invest in.

Degiro and Other Brokers Fees Comparison

	DEGIRO	Hargreaves Lansdown	Barclays	ii	Halifax	HSBC	Average cost of competitors mentioned	Your savings with DEGIRO
Tesco for £1,000	£1.89	£11.95	£6.00	£7.99	£12.50	£10.50	£9.99	81%
Vodafone for £5,000	£2.45	£11.95	£6.00	£7.99	£12.50	£10.50	£9.99	76%
Royal Dutch Shell for £10,000	£3.15	£11.95	£6.00	£7.99	£12.50	£10.50	£9.99	68%
Bank of Ireland for £1,000	£3.86	£11.95	-	£19.99	£12.50	£29.95	£18.98	80%
Nestlé for £2,000	£4.36	£11.95	-	£19.99	£12.50	£29.95	£20.88	79%
BMW for £4,000	£5.36	£11.95	-	£19.99	£12.50	£29.95	£24.68	78%
Apple ($300/share) for	£0.44	£11.95	-	£7.99	£12.50	£29.95	£18.48	

ABOUT THE AUTHOR

Smit Chacha is a writer/author and a stock market investor with over 10 years' experience in the stock market.
With BSc. Computer Visualization and Games degree from London Metropolitan University.

www.ingramcontent.com/pod-product-compliance
Lightning Source LLC
Chambersburg PA
CBHW070904220526
45466CB00005B/2129